A Match Made in Heaven

A Believer's Guide to Getting the Hell Out of Your Marriage

Yvette A. Pete

DEDICATION

To Jesus, the Author and Finisher of my faith.
To my husband, proof that love endures.
To my mom, your support helped make this possible.
To my RLCC Family, thank you for believing in me.

TABLE OF CONTENTS

ACKNOWLEDGMENTS

When God surrounds you with beautiful people, know that you are favored of the Lord. For me, that's the RLCC Sisterhood! You went above and beyond. Thank you!

INTRODUCTION

Are you tired of crying? Of trying? Of dying inside a little more every day you are tethered to what you feel to be the source of your pain? Have you run out of things to say or do to try to fix what has been broken for so long? Do you now feel numb when you see him or her? Have you determined that the only way to cease the pain is to sever the tie? I've been there. And it was hell. Some would say that's harsh, but what is hell? A place of torment...inescapable, continual, intentional torment where you are at the mercy of torturers and there is no hope of reprieve. That pretty much sums up how I felt in the early part of my marriage.

When I initially began this book many, many years ago, I had already gone through almost six years of heartbreak and disappointment with a man who vowed to love, honor and cherish me, but I felt did everything but. I was saved, sanctified, Holy Ghost filled and fire-baptized, so how could I have missed God? I had asked God who my husband was. Had God lied to me? Was God willing to sacrifice me for this man?

The title, *A Match Made in Heaven*, came to me because I pictured a lit match burning up my marriage certificate. I was out; I was done. If this was God's will, I wanted no part of it. I needed to get the hell out. And I was going to tell the world what my husband had done, how all that crap about happily ever after was a fallacy and how God really didn't seem to care about his people, least of all me. I had done my best to love God and be faithful to Him, and I really had tried to love my husband. I was so wounded and disillusioned by my marriage that I began to think that everything I knew about love, marriage, God and family was all a lie.

However, at that time, I couldn't write this book. God wouldn't let me. He wouldn't let me pen poison to page. He wouldn't allow me to write this story from the abyss in which I was. So, the book sat for years until after my healing and restoration. Then He told me, "Write the book. Keep the title. Tell them how to get the hell out, and let Me in."

This book is intended to 1) reveal God's plan for married couples, 2) expose destructive tactics the enemy has for marriage and 3) encourage *believers* to trust in God and his divine plan for them and their spouse despite the hellish trials they may be going through even right now. Reading this book will challenge your sensibilities and may incite your cynicism with every page you read.

This book advocates faith in God and His divine intervention in your life. You will be pushed beyond your imagination and urged to buy in to God's choices for your life according to the Word of God, because He created you, and there's nothing too hard for Him. Did Jesus not turn water to wine? Did He not raise the dead? He is certainly able to redeem even the most horrid marriage from Hades! Trust me, I know! Okay, so I reiterate, this book is only for believers (hence the title) who want to submit to the will of God despite the adversities they face, even when it's dealing with painful revelations and matters of the heart. And since you are still reading, I trust that you believe, and that is the first thing necessary to receive your miracle!

~~~~~~~~~~~~~~~~~~~~~~~~~~~~~~~

For the believing wife brings holiness to her marriage, and the believing husband brings holiness to his marriage. Otherwise, your children would not be holy, but now they are holy. (But if the husband or wife who isn't a believer insists on leaving, let them go. In such cases the believing husband or wife is no longer bound to the other, for God has called you to live in peace.) Don't you wives realize that your husbands might be saved because of you? And don't you husbands realize that your wives might be saved because of you?

1 Corinthians 7:14-16 (NLT)

1 | PUNCH THAT PUNK!

The devil is wreaking havoc on marriages. He is destroying the family structure as ordained by God and making a mockery of Christian values. He is determined to pervert the sanctity of holy matrimony and strategizes ways to destroy the love between husband and wife. Divorce is the devil's way of:

- undermining God's authority in the lives of married Christians,
- causing breaches in the body of Christ,
- exposing future generations to curses and chaos and
- making fools out of God's children.

The sad thing is...many Christians are letting the enemy run roughshod over them and basically operate unchecked! Let it be understood. God gave us power over all the power of the devil, so how can the devil do what he is doing? Because of the hardness of Christians' hearts. Consider Matthew 19:3-8:

The Pharisees also came unto him, tempting him, and saying unto him, Is it lawful for a man to put away his wife for every cause? And he answered and said unto them, Have ye not read, that he which made them at the beginning made them male and female, and said, For this cause shall a man leave father and mother, and shall cleave to his wife: and they twain shall be one flesh? Wherefore they are no more twain but one flesh. What therefore God hath joined together, let not man put asunder. They say unto him, Why did Moses then command to give a writing of divorcement, and to put her away? He saith unto them, Moses because of the hardness of your hearts suffered you to put away your wives: but from the beginning it was not so.

When you marry, you make a vow to love, honor and cherish your spouse till death, but when issues and troubles that seem insurmountable arise, some too quickly give up and throw in the towel. Their hearts become hardened. They are not willing to forgive and trust again. They do not want to be healed and delivered by God. They want out! I get it! I got married in 1998, and by 2004, I had had enough. But the bible says it is better not to make a vow than to make a vow and break it. It also encourages us to not allow our mouth to cause our flesh to sin (Ecclesiastes 5:5-6). Yes, that's what the bible calls it...SIN! "For whatsoever is not of faith is sin" (Romans 14:23). Way too often, individuals are marrying and when trials arise, one or both spouses begin to feel like it is more trouble than it is worth. There are commitment issues, not only to each other, but also to God. They really don't believe God can heal them AND their union. In marriage, the individuals make vows to love, honor and cherish each other, but hurts, infidelities, bitterness and other trials keep couples apart. The sad reality is that not only does such negativity go against the will of God, but it compromises the family foundation and exposes each spouse and any children to the adversary. Husbands and wives become annoyed with each other. They are angry and tired of each other and become indifferent to one another. The bible says that the tongue "is an unruly evil, full of deadly poison" (James 3:8) and "it is set on fire of hell" (James 3:6). Because of the poison of hurt, words are spoken and deeds are done to destroy the other spouse, causing deeper, presumably unhealable wounds. It seems that all hell breaks loose in the marriage. Dear children, a house divided cannot stand! Consider James 4:1-2 and 5-7 which states:

> *From whence come wars and fightings among you? Come they not hence, even of your lusts that war in your members? Ye lust, and have not; ye kill,*

> *and desire to have and cannot obtain; ye fight and war, yet ye have not, because you ask not....Do ye think that the scripture saith in vain, the spirit that dwelleth in us lusteth to envy? But he giveth more grace. Wherefore, he saith, God resisteth the proud, but giveth grace unto the humble. Submit yourselves therefore to God. Resist the devil, and he will flee from you.*

Sometimes in marriage, it feels like everything is falling apart. Spouses don't know how to communicate with one another. When they talk, they are arguing. Instead of the joy and peace of God that should be present, there is devastation and destruction. You get to the point where you don't like the person you married...you feel like you have wasted your time AND your love. Allowing unforgiveness to continue can breed hate, bitterness, murder, strife, and infidelity. It is amazing how happy and hopeful couples are while dating or engaged, but once married, they have little patience with each other. And instead of cleaving to one another, they selfishly resort to the single mentality of *I, me and my*. They sabotage their marriage (because it's failing anyway), and they look for loopholes in the covenant they made with their spouse and God. But God hates the putting away (Malachi 2:16). Marriage is meant to be an example of Christ and the church (Ephesians 5:32). Christ has not and WILL NOT EVER give up on his church. Have you asked God to heal YOU and your marriage? Are you willing to accept your fault in its failure? Have you repented to God for your unbelief and rebellion? If Jesus healed the sick, cast out devils and raised the dead, He can also reconnect spouses, restore the bonds of love and peace and deliver marriages from the fires of hell.

Ladies and gentlemen, you are fighting the wrong enemy! Your spouse is not your enemy, though they may be behaving AS your enemy. Refocus your eyes on the real adversary—the devil, Satan, that old snake—and punch that punk in the face! Remember, "we wrestle not against flesh and blood, but against principalities, against powers, against the rulers of the darkness of this world, against spiritual wickedness in high places" (Ephesians 6:12). Satan is so adept at operating under the radar that it allows him to infiltrate home after home and marriage after marriage. He is a master deceiver and manipulator, so we must recognize him BEFORE he gets to us, BEFORE he can cause havoc. You can do this through prayer! "Watch and pray, that ye enter not into temptation: the spirit indeed is willing, but the flesh is weak" (Matthew 26:41).

According to *Oxford Languages* online, to watch means to look at or observe attentively over a period of time. Marriages can't run on autopilot. You cannot turn a blind eye to things that are not right. You cannot have the mindset that things will right themselves. When you pray, you are keeping your finger on the pulse of your life, your marriage and anything that pertains to you. If something is out of whack, God will not only reveal it to you, but will give you wisdom and strategies as to how to make it well again. Your marriage is worth saving! And you have the Savior!! So why think that He is willing to save the whole world, but would allow your marriage to go up in smoke? I can recall that scripture in Matthew 27:42 when Jesus hung on the cross and revilers mocked him saying, "He saved others, himself he cannot save." That's the thought process of some, that God saved them but cannot save their marriage. We must be like that man who had the son who was demon-possessed and say "Lord, I believe; help thou my unbelief" (Mark 9:24). The temptation is to let things play out according to the devil's plan. This is when you find yourself saying "It's too hard! I can't take it anymore! I've tried to make it work but...!" That's that corruptible flesh talking! It doesn't want to fight. It wants to tuck tail and run away.

So, you see the devil and your flesh get in cahoots against you, to beat your spirit man down. To defeat you! To destroy you and everything that pertains to you! But resist the devil! Tell your flesh, "As for me and my house, we will serve the Lord" (Joshua 24:15). Through the Holy Ghost, we have power to speak things that are not as though they were (Romans 4:17). We have power "over all the power of the enemy"

(Luke 10:19). The bible says that "the kingdom of heaven suffereth violence, and the violent take it by force" (Matthew 11:12). This means that its time out for being on the defensive and not the offensive. We must take the fight to the devil and stop letting him walk all over us. Take authority in your life, your home, your marriage. Have dominion as God already gave you. War in prayer till all aligns to God's will. And keep praying until you knock that punk out! Pray until the peace of God keeps your heart and mind. Pray until the only one packing their bags is the devil!

2 | IT STARTED IN THE GARDEN

As a little girl, I remember playing mommy with my baby dolls and playing with toy kitchens and Easy-Bake Ovens. I remember my mother buying me Barbie dolls, and I also had Barbie's Dream House and Barbie Corvette and, of course, the Ken doll to make the set complete. I remember Snow White and Cinderella stories where the kind, yet troubled princesses got their princes in the end. As I got older, I read romance novels, because I believed in happily ever after. My mother did not say these words to me, and her prince had come and gone---my parents divorced when I was one---but for many of us, we were raised, however inadvertently, through toys, TV, movies or music, to expect that our prince was out there somewhere! Yes, he will come riding on a white horse (for some, it may be in a Pinto). He will deliver us from our troubles, and we will live happily ever after! This is typical in fairy tales, but if you have lived a while, if you are married or have been married, you know already that life is not a fairy tale…far from it!

So, what's the deal? Why are we women so romantically inclined? Why are we seemingly wired to desire the man of our dreams? Why are we dreaming about THE ONE long before we ever meet him? Well, I think the best way to understand this is to go all the way back to the beginning in the garden of Eden with Adam and Eve. Concerning mankind, God made the male first. In Genesis 2, we find that God creates man, places him in the garden and gives him a job: "And the Lord God took the man and put him into the garden of Eden to dress it and to keep it" (Genesis 2:15). Adam's job was to tend (take care of) it and watch over (govern) it. Ladies, please allow me to digress here and say that before you get hooked up with someone, make sure he has a job/career. I understand a man may fall on hard times but not ALL the time. If he has a pattern of quitting or job hopping or is out of work more than he is working, then keep it moving! If a man does not work, he should not eat (2 Thessalonians 3:10). How can he take care of you if he can't take care of himself? Now I know this statement may rankle some women, because they don't need a man to take care of them; they can take care of themselves. Or men may say the woman needs to work too. Lol I got you! But I'm speaking more about God's familial order. The man is the head and thereby must work to provide for the family. The woman's first work is to tend to the home and children. So, chill out! I'm not advocating women sitting on their behinds all day while their husbands work themselves into an early grave. Because of the times in which we live, both spouses should seek God for his wisdom and be agreed regarding what is best for THEIR family, but God's order was set in the garden. He's more than able to provide for us despite the times. The bible admonishes us to not be unwise, but to understand what God's will is (Ephesians 5:17).

Okay, back to the garden. Adam was to have dominion (authority) over God's creation—the garden, the animals, everything! Adam was a busy guy. The wonderful thing is he communed with God daily. I have to say this. In the presence of the Lord is fullness of joy (Psalm 16:11). The keyword is fullness. God is our all-in-all. He is total completeness and sufficiency. There is no want or lack in Him or with Him. Adam was not lonely and pining for someone. He was not complaining that he didn't have anybody. He was not sexually frustrated. He had God! He was perfectly content with his life because he was amid perfection in the presence of God! If you notice in Genesis 2:18, it is God that takes note of and chooses to end Adam's singleness: "And the Lord God said, It is not good that the man should be alone; I will make him a help meet for him."

Now, the next two verses I find absolutely hilarious! Let's look again at what God says in Genesis

2:18 and then continue:

> *And the Lord God said, It is not good that the man should be alone; I will make him a help meet for him. And out of the ground the Lord God formed every beast of the field, and every fowl of the air; and brought them unto Adam to see what he would call them: and whatsoever Adam called every living creature, that was the name thereof. And Adam gave names to all cattle, and to the fowl of the air, and to every beast of the field; but for Adam there was not found a help meet for him.*

God brought out the beasts! He wanted to give Adam a helper, so he presents him with various beasts and fowl to see what Adam would call them. Hmmm...this is a learning lesson for men everywhere. Watch what comes your way and be careful what you call it! This was a test for Adam. Having communed daily with the Lord, Adam had to have been enlightened as to God's intentions. Psalm 84:11 states: "No good thing will he withhold from them that walk uprightly". The bible also reminds us that "if any of you lack wisdom, let him ask of God, that giveth to all men liberally, and upbraideth not; and it shall be given him" (James 1:5). Adam had an all-access pass to the Master of the Universe. Adam correctly saw the animals for what they were…animals! They were not made in the image of God. There was no recognition of character or purpose similar to Adam's own. They were beneath him (remember, he has dominion). There are many women who are hungry for a man, and who are willing to do whatever it takes to have one. They behave as carnivorous beasts or, in our vernacular, man-eaters. Adam was wise enough to avoid the beasts. They were incompatible to him; they could not help him but only hinder him. And note that he did not find a help meet AMONG them. He didn't see anything special amid the zoo. No, the right one for him was sanctified (set apart/singled out) just for him. Check out what God does in Genesis 2:21-23:

> And the Lord God caused a deep sleep to fall upon Adam, and he slept: and he took one of his ribs and closed up the flesh instead thereof; and the rib, which the Lord God had taken from man, made he a woman, and brought her unto the man. And Adam said, This is now bone of my bones, and flesh of my flesh; she shall be called Woman, because she was taken out of Man.

Proverbs 18:22 explains, "*Whoso findeth a wife findeth a good thing, and obtaineth favour of the Lord.*" The man is blessed for his great find! She came out of him, and both agreed that they belong together. They were already "connected" before they met face-to-face. Come on, God! This beautiful process for us is convoluted by carnality and deceptions of the enemy to cause us to bond with a beast. The intention is to abort God's blessing and promises in the lives of mankind. To be honest, that's a bible class all by itself. Are you a beast or are you a blessing?

This is a great segue to why men and women might want a divine hook-up. In simple terms, we desire our soul match. We long for that connection, that since of being where we belong. I must be clear. Man is, by no means, a substitute for God. "God is a Spirit: and they that worship him must worship him in spirit and in truth" (John 4:24). No, I'm talking about a God-ordained, divinely designed, earthly partnership. Marriage is God's way of showing us the importance of covenant relationships, the necessity of the procreation of man and the blessing of obedience in the earth. We need God to help us find our soul match. You may be wondering why I don't use the term soul mate. Well, I still could, but I think the term has gotten a bad rap and has been mistakenly thought to mean one specific person for you and that's it. However, there are times when an individual's spouse dies, and one may remarry in the Lord (1 Corinthians 7:8-9). They must pray and ask God who to marry, but the intended must be saved. They cannot marry an unbeliever.

The term used in Genesis refers to a help that is meet (or sufficient) for Adam. She matches him intellectually, morally, and characteristically (what he needs for balance) to compliment the man and to fulfill their unified destiny. God caused a deep sleep to come over Adam, and He removed one rib from him and made the woman. He then presented her to Adam, who declares her to be "bone of my bones, and flesh of my flesh" (Genesis 2:23) or as modern man might say with help from The Temptations, "My Girl". Please keep in mind that this is Adam who has been in the presence of God daily and who has been trusted with dominion over God's creation. Adam did not look at the size of her breasts or hips or lips. There was no carnality in this recognition, but a soul connection, an identification of something deeper that reminded him of himself. The woman also recognized this connection as she consented to abide with him. She could have chosen to run along after the animals that had come before her, but she stayed with her man.

I believe this love connection is legitimately desired by most men and women. Considering Adam and Eve's experience and the fact that God hand-crafted one individual for another, God established a precedent that day that continues till present day. We should not be blindly grasping for whatever comes our way but seeking God for the truth of His will for our life. In this way, we will discover the match with whom God commanded us to "be fruitful and multiply and replenish the earth" (Genesis 1:28). Remember, it is a command of God. It is also God's desire that we raise up children "in the nurture and admonition of the Lord" (Ephesians 6:4). To do this, both parties must have a relationship with the Lord, and both must accept the responsibility of training the children up in the way they should go, trusting that when they are old, they will not depart from it (Proverbs 22:6). To have a godly lineage, the parents must be godly. And for that matter, the marriage/family must be built on a godly foundation. It is not popular, but God's Word is the ultimate authority—holy matrimony is to be between a man and a woman--ONE man and ONE woman. God's ordinance for marriage was established in the garden, and He has not changed it. The Bible also tells us in 1 Corinthians 7:14: "For the unbelieving husband is sanctified by the wife, and the unbelieving wife is sanctified by the husband: else were your children unclean; but now are they holy." This speaks to a godly lineage. That is why it is so important to consider who we join ourselves to because our choices affect more than just our life. This is also why the enemy does his best to tear up marriages or deviate us from who God has chosen for us. He wants to snuff out the godly seed!

Adam and Eve were an example to us of God's establishment of a godly union. God made them in his image and likeness, He gave them dominion, He walked with them daily and explained his commandments- you can eat of any tree in the garden but just don't eat of the tree of the knowledge of good and evil in the middle of the garden. In the day you eat of it, you will die. Can't go wrong with that, right? You know the story. They screwed up! Just like we do much of the time. They made poor choices. They listened to the devil. They chose the desire of their flesh. They disobeyed God. Immediately after their selfish decision, they were ashamed (they knew they were naked and tried to cover themselves), they were unrepentant (they blamed others for their deeds), they were displaced from where they should be (they were kicked out of the garden) and they were sentenced to hard labor (the woman would have pains in childbirth and the man would have to till the harsh land and it would not bring forth without sweat.) It's important to say that Adam and Eve were NOT cursed by God. The serpent was. On the contrary, God shed the blood of an animal to cover their nakedness, a precursor of the later sacrifice of the Lamb of God, Jesus Christ! Oh, the grace and mercy of our God!

So, learn from Adam and Eve's mistakes. They had no idea that their selfishness, pride, and disobedience was going to affect them and the generations after them the way it did. They did not understand that death would pass upon all men, "even over them that had not sinned after the similitude of Adam's transgression" (Romans 5:12-14). They did not consider that their sin would open the door for sickness and moral decay to enter the world. They did not fathom that the dominion that they were given over all things, including the very earth upon which they dwelled, would be handed over to that serpent, Satan. That's how sin is. It will cost you and those around you. Is God at fault because he did not keep the enemy from them? Absolutely not! He gave them dominion, just like he has given it to you. I could say that they did not have prior examples to help them to know what to do since they were the first couple. But they had God! They had already been given God's blessing, dominion, authority and presence, but they gave it all away. What are you about to give away?

3 | THE POLLUTION OF FORNICATION

Now I must reiterate that holy matrimony is divinely designed, orchestrated and sanctioned by God. Thereby compliance cannot be optional for the child of God. According to the world, you don't have to marry, and you can have as much sex as you want with whomever you want. You can shack up and have children without the hassle of a binding document, or you can have many children from multiple partners and yet be free to continue to sow elsewhere. This is not the will of God!

The Bible admonishes us to escape from fornication (1 Corinthians 6:18). The earth is polluted with the sin of fornication. Why do I say that? Let's look at the definition of fornication. According to *Oxford Languages*, fornication is "sexual intercourse between people not married to each other". Pollution is "the presence in or introduction into the environment of a substance or thing that has harmful or poisonous effects". Fornication is rooted in spiritual rebellion. It flies in the face of God's covenant of marriage and gives precedent to the lust of one's flesh. The bible says that "man is tempted when he is drawn away of his own lust and enticed. Then lust when it conceives it brings forth sin and sin when it is finished, it brings forth death" (James 1:14-15). This is reiterated by 1 John 2:16 when it states that "all that is in the world is the lust of the flesh, lust of the eye and the pride of life." This can be seen as three separate events of lust, or as a descent into the rabbit hole of fleshly depravity. In other words, sin getting exceeding sinful. It starts with the lust of the flesh (being desirous of something outside of God), then it leads down to lust of the eye (seeing an access point to what you desire and pursuing it), which leads to the pride of life (attaining your desire and thinking it's okay, that you can do whatever you want). So, with each person and each circumstance, lust keeps conceiving and bringing forth. What do these fornication babies look like? Inwardly, they look like defilement, deception, vanity, manipulation, religion, witchcraft and derision for God's authority. Outwardly, they manifest as perverse choices like promiscuity, pedophilia, homosexuality, molestation, orgies, bestiality, masturbation and adultery. God commands us to be holy and separated from worldly mentalities, but the cycle continues and worsens through each generation. This is how the earth has been polluted with fornication. We now live in an age of sexual freedom and exploration. But it is undermining God's family structure and eroding the sacredness of godly families. Think about it! Homosexuals copulate with the same sex, thereby halting natural procreation. The promiscuous and adulterers practice whoredoms and can have multiple children from ungodly relationships. Orgies, bestiality, pedophilia and molestation are licentious acts condemned by God that destroy families. Masturbation, though acceptable in the world, is sin because it is sex outside the confines of marriage (it is still sin even if you are married), it is with yourself (which can be a gateway to homosexuality), and it cannot bring forth children.

When God destroyed the inhabitants of the earth in the time of Noah, it was because of man's wickedness. Mankind had so absolutely corrupted himself through perpetual sin, rebellion and refusal to turn back to God that it grieved God that he created mankind. In a nutshell, humans became their own God, and each did what he/she felt was right in his/her own sight. They became an ungodly generation, totally souled out to sin. By the time Noah came along, man had polluted the land with unrighteousness and abominations. They had spiraled down to the degree that Sons of God were having sex with the daughters of men. They were choosing as many "wives" as they wanted and with them "creating" a new human hybrid. Genesis 6:5-6 and 11-12 aptly sums up the state of man and God's disappointment with their wickedness and unrepented behavior.

> *And God saw that the wickedness of man was great in the earth, and that every imagination of the thoughts of his heart was only evil continually. And it repented the LORD that he had made man on the earth, and it grieved him at his heart... The earth also was corrupt before God, and the earth was filled with violence. And God looked upon the earth, and, behold, it was corrupt; for all flesh had corrupted his way upon the earth.*

Apostle Paul continually admonished the saints to keep/maintain their vessels: "Know ye not that ye are the temple of God, and that the Spirit of God dwelleth in you? If any man defile the temple of God, him shall God destroy; for the temple of God is holy, which temple ye are" (1 Corinthians 3:16-17). According to *Merriam-Webster.com*, the definition of defile is "to corrupt the purity or perfection of; to make unclean especially with something unpleasant or contaminating". Did you get that? We become contaminated when we sin. Our purity becomes corrupted. Sin personally and adversely affects us. However, fornication is a more grievous and personal offense to God and yourself.

In 1 Corinthian 6:13, we read that "the body is not for fornication, but for the Lord." Further down in 1 Corinthians 6:15-19, it states:

> *Know ye not that your bodies are the members of Christ? Shall I then take the members of Christ, and make them the members of an harlot? God forbid. What? know ye not that he which is joined to an harlot is one body? For two, saith he, shall be one flesh. But he that is joined unto the Lord is one spirit. Flee fornication. Every sin that a man doeth is without the body; but he that committeth fornication sinneth against his own body. What? Know ye not that your body is the temple of the Holy Ghost which is in you, which ye have of God, and ye are not your own?*

Fornication is a sin against your body because you have been unified/joined/fused with the Lord when you received his Spirit. You have become one spirit with him (you are in him by the Spirit; he is in you by the Spirit). Nevertheless, YOU take your body--the members of Christ, your vessel of honor, God's holy sanctuary--and hook up, if you will, with the ungodly to do ungodly deeds. YOU desecrate your temple which means it's no longer sacred! YOU violate it! YOU pollute it! YOU give away your sanctification like a $2 whore…and YOU are the pimp! Newsflash!!! You're not supposed to be on the market anymore!! Therefore, fornication is egregious to God and you. Paul told the saints, "I am jealous over you with godly jealousy: for I have espoused you to one husband, that I may present you as a chaste virgin to Christ" (2 Corinthians 11:2). You should not think your espousal/betrothal to God is inconsequential, any more so than you should think your vow to a natural spouse is inconsequential. Don't come on this side of the cross and continue in former lusts that will breach your relationship with God and, if unchecked, solidify your space in hell.

Where sin remains, corruption will follow. It will tear up your household and can perpetuate in the lives of any offspring because it becomes a generational curse. We must break the cycle of sin. We must invite God back into our lives, into our homes, into our marriages. We must keep our flesh under subjection and resist the temptation to follow anger, hurt, lust, unforgiveness, etc. We cannot allow our families to be corrupted by vile affections and fornications. Carnality is self-destructive. Keep your vessel holy and acceptable to God which is your reasonable service (Romans 12:1). We must do things God's way if we expect them to work out well.

There are two circumstances where individuals do

not marry or have sex. Paul refers to this in 1 Corinthians 7:7-9, "For I would that all men were even as I myself, but every man hath his proper gift of God, one after this manner, and another after that. I say therefore to the unmarried and widows, it is good for them if they abide even as I. But if they cannot contain, let them marry: for it is better to marry than to burn". This is where the term *gift of celibacy* is derived. Paul had this gift. Prophetess Anna in Luke 2:36-37 had this gift. And of course, John the Baptist and Jesus were gifted with celibacy. In cases of this gift, individuals do not marry and remain virgins or choose to remain sexually inactive once their spouse has passed. This was the case with Prophetess Anna. Such gifted souls choose celibacy that they may devote themselves to the service of God. Are you choosing celibacy if you are gifted to be celibate? Well, think about it. It does not mean that they had no temptation or physical desire to have sex, but they maintained self-control. In the scripture it says, "if they cannot contain". You do not have this gift if you cannot NOT have sex. This includes masturbating which is sexual self-gratification.

Having sex before marriage can lead to a lot of trouble connecting with your new spouse. You have made connections — soul ties--with however many others, and this can hinder you from making a connection with your husband or wife now that you are saved and living for God. God says that marriage is honorable and the bed undefiled. But wouldn't getting in bed with multiple partners be perverse? Yes! So, we must have those soul ties broken. Again, the thought is that the salvation process has delivered us already. It has. But we have left so many doors open to the enemy for his return when, as I stated before, our mind is not renewed. We must break Satan's hold on us (he wants to take control of you again). Renounce former ideals and mindsets. Dedicate your mind, body and soul to God!

Ever heard of triggers? A smell, a place, and a particular song that you hear? These can be triggers to remind you of former times with former people. And when we are vulnerable and hurting, it is tempting to go back to the dumb stuff that we left long ago. Have you ever known someone to have gotten out of a bad relationship and is doing well (whether with another person or not), but when hard times come, they end up back with the person with whom they had a toxic relationship? You may scratch your head to such perceived foolishness, but soul ties, open doors, triggers and lack of commitment to God can lead you down such a path. Some, despite having prayed and waited on their promised spouse, are having adulterous affairs with blasts from their tortured past or with fresh devils who make them feel special. Why? How? This dirty, lying, sinful flesh! Give no place to the devil (Ephesians 4:27). Put no confidence in the flesh (Philippians 3:3). Keep yourself unspotted from the world (James 1:27). If you are a virgin, STAY a virgin! Don't complicate your life with fornication. If you are married, STAY with your spouse! Don't complicate your life with adultery. And leave yourself alone! You should not be masturbating whether virgin, single or married. Pollution can stop with you!

4 | DATING EXPECTATIONS

The term dating doesn't have the same connotation that it did when I was younger. Back then, when someone was dating, they might call you on the phone daily or walk you home from school and carry your books. They might take you to a movie and then bring you back home by curfew. Nowadays, dating means seeing one or multiple individuals for romantic companionship with the option of having sex with any or all of them. I daresay that dating is about the freedom of finding an individual with whom to connect emotionally, mentally and/or sexually. However, dating in the Lord has many differences by comparison. Firstly, saints date with the intent to marry. Instead of dating to see if a person could be marriage material, they are observed at church and at public functions. Their "walk with Christ" is evaluated. If they are not saved, they are not a candidate for dating…period! They need to get to know God first. If a person is wishy-washy and in-

and-out of church, they are not committed to God. If they are not committed to God, they will not commit to you! They are not marriage material, and there is NO dating. James 1:8 declares "a double-minded man is unstable in all of his ways", including in relationships! If the person is observed and is thought to be a good candidate and the interest is mutual, then a conversation occurs with the pastor and an announcement is made before the church. The pastor watches for your soul. Informing the congregation is for congratulatory and accountability purposes.

This may seem to be an "old-school" practice, but I think more churches ought to practice this. It will keep couples out of divorce court later if individuals take time to "watch and pray" before making a decision to date. And then, they should go through couples counseling before tying the knot. Too many times, couples rush into marriage (typically to avoid burning in their flesh), but immediately after the honeymoon, find living together difficult. Should they have gotten married? Paul did say it was better to marry than to burn. Well, Paul was trying to let it be known that a lot of trouble can come from not controlling this flesh! Again, it is better to get to know someone before getting married and not have a boatload of discoveries come out later after the "I do's". The key: COMMUNICATION AND PRAYER.

So then, what can the dating process look like now present day? My advisement is before you seek to date anyone, take into consideration these three vital steps.

#1- <u>Ask God to heal you of all brokenness from your past</u>. This is something all saints should do whether they are seeking to date or not. You need to be healed from old hurts, unforgiveness, bitterness, low self-esteem, and generational curses of stubbornness, pride, slothfulness, even vindictiveness. The bible says in Psalm 51:7 and 10, "Purge me with hyssop and I shall be clean: wash me, and I shall be whiter than snow…Create in me a clean heart, O God; and renew a right spirit within me". You must have a clean heart and a RIGHT spirit to have pure motives and make right choices. This is where the elders used to say, "I don't talk like I used to talk! I don't walk like I used to walk! I don't do what I used to do!" Old things are passed away and all things become new. When you are cleansed, purged, and healed, your desire changes. It is no longer to please self or to do your own thing. It is to please God. Then you can sing that song—"I Know I Been Changed"!

Why is it necessary to heal first? Because as creatures of habit, we are destined to repeat the same mistakes, patterns, thought processes and decisions when we have not had our mind renewed. Remember, you must be renewed in the spirit of your mind (Romans 12:2). If your mind does not change, you will not change. And the baggage that you carried from past relationships, you will bring to any new relationships.

#2- Delight yourself in the Lord. The basis of this step comes from Psalm 37:4. This is essential to every Christian's growth simply because your salvation is based on God's will. And if you don't value God's will or desire, then you will not do what he says. This means Jesus must be Lord of your life. There can be no area of your life that is off limits to him. For you to maintain your healing, you need the Lord! For your desires to remain pure, you need the Lord! Otherwise, your desires will again try to take over, and you will find yourself battling between wills—yours and God's. However, that means you have come to what James calls a double-mind. In fact, in James 1:6-8 says, "For he that wavereth is like a wave of the sea driven with the wind and tossed. For let not that man think that he shall receive any thing of the Lord. A double-minded man is unstable in all his ways". Yes, the unstable ways are reminiscent of how you were in the past. You don't want to go back to the past; that's what you were saved from. How do we prevent this battle of wills? Let's look at James 4:7-8 for the answer: "Submit yourselves therefore to God. Resist the devil, and he will flee from you. Draw nigh to God, and he will draw nigh to you. Cleanse your hands, ye sinners; and purify your hearts, ye double minded".

Delighting yourself in the Lord also includes working diligently for the Lord in whatever capacity that He deems and doing what you do heartily as unto God. We are here to be lights and witnesses for God and to serve him. Paul consistently declared that he was a slave to God, meaning God was his master and whatever God wanted, that's what he was going to do! Like Paul, we must be of a mind that whether you are teaching, preaching, doing mission work, singing, ushering, emailing, cooking, cleaning, whatever it is, do it well and with a right spirit for the Lord's sake.

#3 – Ask God to sharpen your discernment. This may seem like an odd request, but you will need to discern the good from the bad and the ugly. If you have truly followed Steps 1 and 2 from your heart, then trust me, Ladies, gentlemen callers will start coming out of the woodwork. Why? Because you are not focused on men but on God, and you are not a lady in waiting but a lady who waits on (serves) her Lord. And, Brothers, ladies will want to capture your attention through flirting or coyness or will want to consistently bend your ear about cars or sports or other issues they think you might be interested in. You will meet all kinds of women that are meant to be distractions and decoys, but you must be able to righteously judge each encounter. This does not mean that you should hurt anyone's feelings or call them wanton and thirsty, but that you take mental notes and listen for God's voice with each individual. The bible states you shall know them by their fruits (Matthew 7:16). Another scripture advises us to know them that labor among you (1 Thessalonians 5:12). There are two Greek words for discernment—*anakrino* which means to examine or judge closely, and *diakrino* which means to separate out, to examine, and to investigate.

You can ask God to tell you who your husband or wife is, or, praise God, you can ask him to let you know who is not! I will say this much, stay in the presence of God. The bible says he will keep your feet from falling (Psalm 116:8). If you choose on our own, then you will choose based on a former frame of reference which is an invitation to hellish conditions. Don't do it! Always trust what God has chosen for you and trust Him to bring the right person in due season.

I want to reiterate how important it is to follow these steps. Step 1 will help bigtime with Step 2. Do all three, and you should be good! Before dating, I did not follow these steps. I learned the hard way through trial and error. But hopefully, with me writing this book, you will have a way better experience than I did. For me, I had a few individuals who were interested, but I shooed them away, because I did not feel they were for me. In all honesty, I was looking more at the outer appearance than from a spiritual standpoint. I would ask myself "Can you see yourself with this person for the rest of your life. Do we match?" The real question was if I was attracted to them or not. If the answer was no, then I moved on. If I saw someone I liked or thought was handsome, I would observe them, to see how they were around others and how they labored in the house of God. If I observed anything—unkindness, bad manners, obnoxiousness, laziness, arrogance, femininity, sin, etc.—I checked them off my list. I know that makes me sound like a snob, but I'm not going to lie. My standards were high, way high. I wanted the best, because I wanted the fairytale. Isn't that what I should expect from the God of my salvation? The perfect love story...the stuff of dreams?! It's what I wanted, and I just knew God was going to give that to me. So, I waited for it. I waited for the *this is the one* moment. There were various interested individuals throughout the years, but none were the one. I even had a mom corner me in a closet at church on behalf of her son, but I told her and him "Sorry, but no!" I had this thing in my head of how all this dating stuff should go, but it was nothing like what I expected.

5 | MY CHOICE VS. GOD'S CHOICE

At 25 years old, I was tired of waiting, but I had settled into a routine of working on my job and serving in the house of God. I ignored my internal clock and chose to trust God that I would not be convalescing somewhere in a nursing home when my husband came for me. Around this time, I was the youth president at my church, and our young people were active and on fire for the Lord. When we would have youth services, youth from all around the community would come and pack out the house, and we would be worshiping and praising God till all hours. We saw such a mighty move of the Holy Ghost. It was an amazing time!

So, it was not a surprise that a friend from the church invited her brother to come up from Louisiana to stay. He was 19 years old and unsaved and, if the Lord didn't intercede, was on his way to jail. His name was Benjamin. When I first met him, I shook his hand in greeting and didn't give him another thought. Eventually the Lord saved him. He fit right in with the other youth and quickly set himself apart as a leader. He rose in ranks to eventually become the VP of the youth department. We spent a lot of time at church and on the phone talking about youth department goals and events and how better to serve the youth in and out of our assembly. It was during these communications that we became friends, best friends. We encouraged each other spiritually and job-wise; we corrected each other when necessary; we supported each other when times got rough, and we always told each other the truth. Even when he let me know he was interested in me romantically, I told him the same thing that I had told others prior to him— "Thanks, but no thanks! I'm waiting on who God has for me." Our friendship continued for two years.

Then one day, our church's youth group was supposed to get together for breakfast. All backed out but the two of us. We laughed and talked about life and our futures over eggs, sausage and toast. Our consensus was that both of us would let our future spouses know that because we were best friends, our families would have to be "best families". We would get houses near each other and raise our kids together and our kids would be play cousins, because there is no way we could live separately of each other. You, as a reader, might think this was strange, but it wasn't strange to us. We loved each other without any of the weird feelings and uncertainties that come with liking somebody. He wasn't trying to get anything from me or play games with me. I didn't have to put on airs with him and pretend to be something I wasn't. It was a perfect friendship! After breakfast, we went to a park, and he pulled out a ring box and asked me to marry him. I was flabbergasted! I couldn't respond. I kept telling him that only my husband was supposed to ask me that. Turns out he was playing a joke on me (there was no ring in the box), but the joke was on both of us. He expected me to say no immediately, but I didn't. I pondered the offer and that gave him hope. For me, I had not thought of him as anything more than my bestie, and now I could not stop thinking about him as my husband.

Needless to say, I had an issue with God. I had asked God who my spouse was and was eagerly awaiting the gentleman's presence. My friend had never been an option. He was six years younger than me. He was not my type. He was 6'3" tall to my 5'1". He was into fishing and hunting; I was into reading and art. Nope. He was not for me. So why was all of this "weird" now going on? The bible says in 1 Corinthians 14:33 that God is not the author of confusion. Well, I was totally confused. I was bothered by the fact that I was bothered by the proposal. I prided myself on being very organized and focused. I concentrated on tasks and saw them through to completion. The present circumstances represented a distraction, a set-back, a set-up of the devil, and so I did what I thought best to clear my mind of the enemy's webs of lies and foolishness. The devil was not going to make a fool of me! I cut off the friendship.

This is a good place to interject that you must be honest with where you are spiritually and naturally. I had a lot of issues, not the least of which was the fact that I felt like I was being duped by God. I got scared. I didn't know what to do. If God was trying to trick me, to trip up my feet, how could I prosper? Well, you know none of this was true. Again, God is not the author of confusion. He most certainly gets no pleasure out of our confusion. Jesus said, "My sheep hear my voice, and I know them, and they follow me" (John 10:27). I thought I knew God's voice. I thought I knew his will, but I was more focused on my own desires. All my romantic expectations were based on my natural deductions. The problem with this is my frame of reference comes entirely from my jacked up past or a romanticized non-reality. I wanted what I felt would be best for me. I prayed for the will of God then proceeded to give Him my list of dos and don'ts and expected Him to miraculously wade through all my mess. I was leaning every bit on my own understanding when the bible tells me in Proverbs 3 not to do so. I wasn't honest with myself regarding my fears. There were three fears that were the motivating factors for my unrealistic list.

1. **I didn't want to divorce**. I told you that my parents divorced when I was one, but I didn't tell you that all my aunts and uncles had divorced. My paternal grandparents stayed married but according to my grandmother, that was a choice made for the sake of her children. There was a generational curse of divorce in my family, and I did not want that for myself. I was afraid it would happen as I did not have any good role models, but I figured if I gave myself the best start possible, maybe the likelihood would decrease. I also did not want my children to experience separation from their father and have to deal with the hole that that leaves in the heart. I spent the better part of my life feeling like my father didn't love me and like I had to prove to him that I was worthy of his love. I got good grades in school, stayed out of trouble, graduated with honors, etc. just to show him that I could be worthy of his love.

2. **I didn't want to be unhappy**. I have no recollection of my mom and dad being together. There are a few photos in boxes but if not for those, I would almost doubt their union. By all intents and purposes, their marriage started off strong but

derailed from dishonesty and infidelities. Gone were the daily flower bouquets and words of love. I can only imagine how heartbroken my mother was--a young wife trying to understand this stranger that was her husband and making a plan of action with two kids that she never expected to raise alone. No, I didn't want that.

3. **I didn't want to be lonely.** I didn't want to have spent so long a time waiting on my Mr. Right only to find out that he was so very wrong. I didn't want to long for someone to share my life with and then after marriage, still feel that sense of loneliness because at the end of the day, they don't want me. They don't want to communicate, and they have other things they'd rather spend their time doing, rather than spending it with me. It came down to my feelings of inadequacy and lack of worth. Could I hold someone's attention for long period of time? This was in reference to my feelings of abandonment by my father. As well too, because none of the relationships I had lasted more than about two years. They all walked away (some I did not regret their departure as they were nothing more than

hell in jeans. But some, when they walked away, it really hurt me.)

These fears fueled my list. They were the reason I was so meticulous in my husband selection. They were the reason I rejected person after person including my best friend. I had unattainable standards and, no doubt, would never have found a worthy candidate. Even the young man I thought was my mate (he shall remain nameless of course). I held him in high regard because I did not know him and thereby was able to imagine that he was perfectly suited to me. He became an idol to me. I could not attain to his "perfection" but hoped that he would be willing to love me despite all my flaws until I could rise to his level. What kind of nonsense is that!? All my days I would have been jumping through hoops, trying to earn his love and feeling very inadequate for having to do so. That's what I felt like I had had to do all my life—become a chameleon so that I could be accepted. And I was willing to put myself in that situation again on this side of the cross. Would God require that of me? The scripture in Jeremiah 29:11 says this: "For I know the thoughts that I think toward you, saith the Lord, thoughts of peace, and not of evil, to give you an expected end". I really had not trusted God to know what was best for me. When you spend so many years making your own choices, good or bad, and dealing with the consequences of said choices, you stick to that because it is familiar.

However, God does not want us to rely on what's familiar to us. That means we are relying on the carnal to make our choices--what we remember from our past. But isn't that what messed us up in the first place? If we were such good judges of character or if we knew what we were doing with our life, we would have no need to come to God in the first place. Even after salvation, some of our mindsets have not changed. We must learn to let this mind be in us that was also in Christ Jesus (Philippians 2:5). We must learn how to walk in the spirit so that we do not fulfill the lusts of the flesh (Galatians 5:16). Our old mindsets were busted mindsets. They were broken; they were flawed. If we are not purified by the Master and washed of old mindsets, we will welcome hell into any new relationships. We must be changed! God is our deliverer! He really knows what we have need of before we can ask or think it (Ephesians 3:20). Before He blesses, He prepares the space to receive the blessing! He allows you to see yourself, in the raw, in the ugly. He allows us to see/feel what is not right so that we can ask Him to fix what's wrong. I asked God to help me. But I still had trouble trusting Him. I held on to my fears. I held on to my defenses. I thought I knew God, but I didn't really. The day we come to God our hearts are open to Him, to receive his love. But sadly, we have been living in the natural realm for so long, worldly ways are embedded in us. We must learn to walk in our regeneration. We must learn to incline our ears to the voice of God and follow after his ways even when it makes no sense to our carnal mind. The bible says in 1 Corinthians 2:12-14:

> [12] *Now we have received, not the spirit of the world, but the spirit which is of God; that we might know the things that are freely given to us of God.*
>
> [13] *Which things also we speak, not in the words which man's wisdom teacheth, but which the Holy Ghost teacheth; comparing spiritual things with spiritual.*
>
> [14] *But the natural man receiveth not the things of the Spirit of God: for they are foolishness unto him: neither can he know them, because they are spiritually discerned.*

We cannot follow God with our natural man in control. For real, we are not following God when we walk in the flesh and lean to our own familiar understanding. We are leading the way and blazing a trail straight to hell. God wants us to surrender all. "We are his people and the sheep of his pasture" (Psalm 100:3). He is raising us up in righteousness, but we must surrender our will to him in every way. This is not always simple because we are creatures of habit, of familiarity. We want to be in control. But thank God for his grace and mercy seeing us through daily. His patience keeps us from destructive ways and decisions that will adversely affect us for the long term.

I had to trust God with every part of my heart. I can say it was easier said than done. Fear of failure is real and understandable, but it is not of God. Fears can skew your choices and make you miss out on all that God has for you. And we never have to be afraid of God's choices for our life. Every good and perfect gift comes from him (James 1:7). If you rely on your choices, you're going to get what you've always gotten — lost!

6 | YOU DO THE "I DO"!

Saying "I do" is one of the happiest moments in an individual's life. You have found someone with whom you want to spend the rest of your days. They bring you joy. You have connected on a mental and emotional level. You can't imagine your life without them. Some would dare say "You complete me!" to their newly wedded spouse, riding on the romantical wings of the glorious day. Then there's the honeymoon, where you lawfully get to express your love and devotion to your mate as often and as many times as you like.

Marriage can be everything it's meant to be, but some have put more emphasis on the wedding or the fact of being married than in being honest about the person with whom they are making a vow. Oftentimes long before the engagement or the nuptials, there are what I like to call flags on the play. Does the person have a relationship with Jesus? (That should always be question #1). Are they compassionate? Are they a giver? Do they like to work, cook, clean? Do they pay their tithes? Do they have friends outside of you? What kind of friends do they have (birds of a feather...)? Can you randomly ask for their unlocked phone, and they give it without hesitancy? Do they like your family? Do you like theirs? Do you trust this person? A lot of times we override our natural instincts just to have someone. We can know that they are not the best choice, but we'll take them AS IS because we are broken. We want to be taken AS IS, so we take whatever we get. Let me explain what I mean. Because we long for love but are insecure and emotionally unstable, we'll accept ideals and behaviors that are not good for us. If we're honest, we'll acknowledge the fact that we carry baggage from past relationships into the marriage and as soon as an infraction occurs, we retreat into that place of brokenness. The person is not responsible for our happiness, but we sure make them feel like they are. That's a lot of pressure on a brother or sister! Of course, your spouse should make you want to be a better person, but if you're starting off at a love deficit, no one can dig you out of that hole. Only God can fulfill you! Only He can satisfy you! Nothing and nobody can make you whole but God. Happiness is short lived when you expect another human to fill a void in you. You jump at the chance to be married, because you've known so much rejection. You give or take the offered ring even though there have been more arguments than apologies. You think this time it's real though you're actually afraid that it's not. Why do you do that? L-O-V-E!! You want it and need it; you just don't know what it is. Sadly, you rely heavily on your frame of reference which will mislead you every time, because it's rooted in the love sickness of your past. Because you don't recognize real love, you fall for the decoy. You marry for better or worse and worse comes right out the gate. Fighting, lies, cheating, defenses, unforgiveness, and feelings of betrayal come, and you feel duped and wounded and alone, because your marriage is failing. You are heartbroken. How did it get here? Well, it started before the ceremony!

In God's math, two halves make one half, but one whole plus one whole equal one whole. You must be whole before joining yourself to another. You need healing from generational curses, misguided ideals, emotionalism, fears and brokenness. You need the Lord to purge you of unrighteousness. If you can't receive love from God, you're not likely to receive it when it comes from a good man or woman, because you will flow with what's familiar to you which is taint not truth. So, what happens if you've joined yourself to another broken soul? One of two things. God can save your marriage, or YOU can let it die! According to Malachi 2:16, God hates the putting away. The Bible also states that he is married to the backslider (one who has turned back from what is right) and that God has called us to dwell in peace.

If you submit your will to God and pray and are willing to be healed and do not harden your heart, God can preserve/renew your marriage. In such a case, WAIT, WATCH and PRAY. Follow God's directives, and don't allow discouragement to set in. The other party must do the same. If both of you submit (you can't make or coerce them into it), your marriage will be saved because love never fails (1 Corinthians 13:8). However, if you submit yourself to God and do all that I mentioned before and God (and I reiterate GOD) makes a way of escape for you (because of the other spouse's lack of submission), take it. That doesn't mean run to divorce court but to let God order your steps. The Bible states in 1 Corinthians 7:15, "if the unbelieving depart, let him depart."

I must stress that you must seek God for his direction and be willing to say yes to Him. He sees the thoughts and intents of your heart, so you can't pull one over on Him. He said if you are married, do not seek to be loosed (1 Corinthians 7:27). You can't just want to get out of a bad marriage that your partly responsible for being in just to go your way and do your thing. There are so many jacked up people out there who were just as responsible for the breakdown of their marriage, but they won't own up to it and they refuse to change. They want a do-over but not with the current spouse who is willing to work things out. They don't want to humble themselves. They don't want to put in the work it takes to have a successful marriage. They don't want God's way but want to continue in their own ways, leaving casualties behind them. This is not a game of musical spouses--don't like this one, just get another one! In this way, you perpetuate the cycle of sin and brokenness and drag any children through the hell of your life. It has to stop!! Submit yourself to God and he will lift you in due season. Trust him with your heart!

7 | A MATCH MADE IN HEAVEN

There is a scripture in Matthew 6:10 that reads-"Thy kingdom come. Thy will be done in earth, as it is in heaven". Thy will be done, Lord, down here as it already is up there. Does that mean anything to you? Does it resonate as it should with the people of God? I don't think so. Paul said in 1 Corinthians 3:1-3:

> **3** *And I, brethren, could not speak unto you as unto spiritual, but as unto carnal, even as unto babes in Christ.*

> **2** *I have fed you with milk, and not with meat: for hitherto ye were not able to bear it, neither yet now are ye able.*

> **3** *For ye are yet carnal: for whereas there is among you envying, and strife, and divisions, are ye not carnal, and walk as men?*

Paul sounded annoyed! Why? Because we were missing something. Remember, he is not talking to the unsaved, those who think spiritual things are foolish. No, he was talking to the church and telling them, "You are babies! Immature, whiny little babies!" Paul wanted to offend our sensibilities to incite righteous indignation of our own carnal behavior. We can't receive truth like God wants to give it to us. It reminds me of Jack Nicholson's character in *A Few Good Men* (Reiner) when he was being interrogated by Tom Cruise's character. Tom says, "I want the truth!" and Jack responds emphatically, "You can't handle the truth!" Yep, this is what Paul is saying here. The truth makes us free. We've come to God, and we are glad we came, but that's it. We want to take it from there. We want the creature comforts of our life to continue even if that means we keep living a lie. We'd rather pretend to be children of light than actually be children of light which would require us to dwell in the light of Christ. To walk in truth. To walk in the deliverance of God. To ask God to deliver us from the sins and weights that so easily beset us. To trust him with our life even when we don't see where all this is going to go. We talk a good game. We say all the right things, but our words are hollow. Our actions speak louder than our words.

And what does Paul mean in 1 Corinthians 3:3 when he states: "For ye are yet carnal: for whereas there is among you envying, and strife, and divisions, are ye not carnal, and walk as men?" He means and walk as regular, average, ho-hum, mundane, mediocre unremarkable fleshly and sinful men! As opposed to what? Extraordinary, powerful, fearless, victoriously liberated children of the living God, that's what! We must change to become the manifestation of God's desire! Full of light and life, moving effortlessly in the spirit realm.

I chose my husband, not having the benefit of this wisdom. I do not advise anyone to do what I did to decide which to choose. I told God okay, you tell me which one is the one I should marry. Both gentlemen had biblical names so I felt it should work. I would toss my bible in the air and wherever it landed, whoever's name was on the page, would be the one. Well, I tossed the bible, and it opened to the scripture in Genesis 35:18: "And it came to pass, as her soul was in departing, (for she died) that she called his name Ben-oni: but his father called him Benjamin". I said, "What! Are you serious!?" I'd love to tell you that that ended all the fears, but it didn't. I didn't have peace like I wanted, because I wondered if it had been a fluke that his name was on the page. Then I felt like crap, because I was doubting. Was my best friend really the one God had chosen for me? I finally talked with Ben. I told him what I did. He was glad, but he was worried about me. He wanted to know if I was happy and asked if I wanted him as my husband. I said I was, but I lied. I was terrified. I was unsure.

What if we were making the biggest mistake of our lives? Coming from a superstitious background, the enemy messed with my mind big time. I kept thinking about the fact that he wasn't what I would have chosen for myself. I kept thinking about the fact that I was older than him naturally and spiritually. I kept thinking about the fact that we were from two totally different backgrounds. I was not country at all. In fact, I would tease him about feeling like it was a modern-day Green Acres situation. I kept thinking about running away, so I would not have to choose.

With all these doubts and fears, the day Ben proposed to me was anything but what I would have had it to be. In anticipation of one day meeting the man of my dreams, I had of course already looked at wedding dresses and rings and thought of how I'd want my wedding to be. I won't get into all the details pertaining to that, but I will discuss the ring. I had studied the 5 c's of a diamond, and I knew I wanted a solitaire. It didn't have to be huge and seen from miles away, but small (not too small) and classic.

When he proposed, he got down on one knee, and told me how much he loved me and asked me to be his wife…and I froze for a moment. I was so scared. I thought to say no out of the sheer terror of saying yes, but I finally was able to say it. When he put the ring on my finger, I hated it instantly. It was big and gaudy and glass. I wrestled with whether to tell him or not. He was so sincere and sweet; I did not want to hurt his feelings. But at the thought of having to wear that ring and show others, I had to say something. I felt bad, but I know I would have felt worse had I not said anything. And I didn't want to embarrass him. He had not studied the 5 c's of a diamond. Why would he? I was the one who had rehearsed this moment for years in my mind. He was unaware that I was taking this situation as a sign that he wasn't the one (again, I had superstitious ways) rather than taking it as his lack of knowledge. When I told him, he was gracious and said he was glad I said something. We went that day to return the glass ring then went to the jeweler and I picked out my own ring. It was a beautiful solitaire with impressive clarity and color that winked often at me. I was happy, but I still had doubts. I had major what-ifs at this time. I loved Ben, but what if I was wrong and the other guy was really my husband? What if this was all a ruse of the devil, and God is talking to me, but I just can't hear him? These were all very real fears that I did not share with my new fiancé. I did not want to hurt him or for him to think that he was not good enough. It was all me and the unrest of my mind.

As you can see, I started off way wrong. I was keeping secrets. I was harboring fears and not seeking God earnestly to take them away. I was not realistic in my expectation of what I wanted because it was based on my past, not on God's promise. Man, looking back as I write this, I was so screwed up. I didn't have anyone to talk to, because those around me had either divorced or were not happy with their current spouse. I didn't talk to my pastor because Ben had gone to him and asked for my hand and pastor had consented. He was happy for us. And who could I talk to about not understanding God's choice for me? Prior to my engagement, I had gone to my pastor to inform him of who I thought my husband was. I trusted my pastor as a man of integrity, and he had never steered me wrong. He told me the other guy was not a good choice, to go back and pray. He did not give details or explain his stance. Well, my pastor should know, I thought. The gentleman himself, though he had shown some interest at times, had not officially declared any affection for me. He had made no attempt to let me know of any intentions toward me. He had not contacted my pastor as far as I knew, and he left no hint that he was ever going to pursue me. I endured this for about a year and a half. So, I could safely let that go, yet I didn't. Again, what if…

The one thing I can say here is from Matthew 6:33: "But seek ye first the kingdom of God, and his righteousness; and all these things shall be added unto you." I began to pray for God to give me peace and clarity. I asked God to cover my mind and help me receive His will in my heart. This was a big step for me, and I had not been down this road before. I had to encourage myself in the Lord and believe that the Lord would not leave me or forsake me. God knew what he was doing, and he knew how to tell me if I was making the biggest mistake of my life. I trusted God to bring me into the fruition of his will.

Now you might be saying, but God is not the author of confusion. And you are right! He is not! I opened myself to confusion when I did not surrender to the will of God and dismiss all my doubts and fears. I did not rebuke the devil so that he would flee from me. I co-signed with him and thereby welcomed the hell and chaos he was offering. You may be saying yes, but God has not given us the spirit of fear, but of power, of love and of a sound mind (1 Timothy 1:7). Correct! However, again, I was walking in the flesh and doing and responding as I would outside of salvation. I was complaining and murmuring and fussing and stressing and allowing myself to be a hot mess, because things were not going the way I wanted them to go. I wanted to be in control, but I very much so was not. I needed to surrender to God. Now, I did say Lord except this be Your will, let this cup pass from me. I'm not crazy. I did not want to be in a relationship where I chose. I knew enough to know that that would be foolish. I just wanted to know that I wasn't so in love with the idea of marriage that I wasn't discerning his divine will. There is a permissive and a divine will of God. Permissive will is when you are making a choice and God permits or allows it to be so. Divine will is totally God's choice and you roll with that. It will take you out of your comfort zone. Your flesh may not agree with it. However, if you humble yourself and submit to it, it will work out exactly like He planned in His mind, and it will be the stuff of heaven. That's what I wanted. So, I prayed...a lot.

Ben and I got married less than two months after he proposed. We figured, why wait when we had already been friends for two years. Also, we did not want to fornicate, though I must confess that we did twice. That was another reason for my emotional upheaval. I felt like I had saved myself for my husband (I was a proud virgin-again, pronounced *ver-jina-gan*) since my salvation, but I didn't wait till he WAS my husband. I felt so bad that I had let Ben, God and myself down. I wanted so badly to be perfect. I later felt like much of the calamity that was my life was me reaping what I had sown.

There were many that were excited for our marriage; some that were against it. Some thought we were rushing it, because I was "secretly pregnant" (I was not). Others who were aware of how long I had waited, rejoiced in our courtship and thought nothing of a short engagement. Even our pastor had consented to and officiated it. When I say the Lord blessed us in abundance for our wedding, I mean it. God had given us favor with so many. Our cake was donated, my dress was donated (including the alterations), and the reception dinner was donated. The bridal party dresses were gorgeous and were purchased at a huge discount. The tuxes for the groomsman were inexpensive with my fiancé's tux being free. The only thing we paid for was the flowers and some wedding supplies. The venue for the wedding and the reception was the church, which our Pastor and First Lady blessed us to use for free. It was a beautiful, candle-lit evening wedding. More than anything, God was present. Everything was going to be alright, right?

8 | HERE COMES THE HELL

I's married now!! I jumped the broom. I took a leap of faith. I said yes. So, what could go wrong? EVERYTHING!! We got married on a Friday in July, honeymooned over that weekend, and my husband, who worked in construction, was laid off couple of weeks later. We lived in a one-bedroom apartment that I had been living in for over four years so not a problem. However, he didn't get another job right away which caused a strain on the finances considering additional utility and food costs. And I found out he wasn't the neatest person (according to my standards) which caused friction since the place was small and he was home all day.

There was another bothersome issue that was troubling our union. My husband really, really, really loved sex...lots of it, as often as possible. Me, I liked it, but wasn't by any means compelled to do it every time I blinked. Although I appreciated his attraction to me and his virility, it became overwhelming. I remember nights where I would be exhausted having gotten up early to go to work, only to come home and have to clean up, make dinner and wash dishes. After cuddling with my hubby while watching a movie, I would get ready for bed, longing to hug the pillow when here comes my new husband wanting my attention. Once was not enough, sometimes twice was not enough. Sometimes it would go on for what felt like hours. I would be exhausted and sore by morning only to come home and be expected to perform again. There were times when I just wanted him to hold me, but most times it had to end in sex. I tried to talk to him about what was going on, but it would lead to hours-long spats about how I didn't really want him. These conversations typically ended with sex in order to appease him. This is where I was talking about how we come to marriage with ideals of what a marriage is, and we can be so far off the mark. My hubby, like me, had little to no good role models for marriage. And we were off to a horrible start.

That December I found out I was pregnant, I got laid off, I had fibroids that were terribly painful so that I couldn't eat, walk or sleep, and I was trying hard not to think I was cursed. I loved my husband. I just didn't know how to live with him. I felt like no matter what I did, I couldn't satisfy him, physically or emotionally. Our communication staggered then stalled. We kept our feelings to ourselves, unless we were fussing at each other. I also made any and every excuse not to have sex with him or obliged him only when I couldn't get out of it. Thus continued the doubts, distrust, lack of understanding and decline of our marriage. We settled into a cordial partnership. We put on a united front at church and in front of others, but when we were alone, the cracks in our façade showed. I do want to say that all our time together was not horrible. We loved each other. We had moments where we allowed ourselves to relax and laugh together. They just got fewer and farther in between. And for me, we could be having a great day, but as the evening loomed and sex perhaps was expected, my defenses went up. For him, that was an act of rejection, which eventually gave him a reason to start having affairs. I betrayed him by my fears and rejection; he betrayed me with adultery and lies. As the years wore on, I allowed myself to become bitter and angry, and I gave in to depression.

I felt like God set me up. Didn't he know all this chaos was going to occur? The fairy tale wasn't real. Happily-ever-after was a myth. I got played. The years had been rough to say the least. In fact, at the time that I received the title of this book, *A Match Made in Heaven*, I pictured a literal match setting fire to my wedding certificate. And the original subtitle, *How to Get the Hell Out of Your Marriage*, was because I wanted to do just that—GET OUT.

I remember when we moved to Louisiana, Ben's

home state. I did not want to go, but I did. I had no money and no means to take care of my two children on my own. Also, I guess I was hoping that God would deliver me, since I had no one but Ben to depend on. My husband was backslidden, and I was holding on by a thread. My husband and I talked about the kids or house business, but seldom anything else. I didn't want to talk to him, and I don't think he knew what to say to me. By then I was trying not to hate him, but I wasn't putting forth much effort. I could hear the enemy telling me to kill him and that would end my troubles, but I knew that was lie. I just couldn't understand why Ben would bring me down to the backside of a desert and leave me by myself. He had his family and friends; I had no one. I couldn't understand why he wouldn't just leave me. Why torture me? Why keep hurting me with lies and affairs? Why would he keep saying he loved me, when by his actions, he hated me?

During that time, God showed Himself faithful. He wouldn't let me stay in a depression. He was always sending a word of healing to me. I remember going to Eunice to go grocery shopping, and I was crying so hard that I almost had to pull over. But I heard "My Life is in your Hands" by Kirk Franklin playing on the radio. Even though I spent most times with just my children, He let me know I was not alone. God really was with me. At this one church, we were over the praise team. God used me to lead the praise team, to exhort the congregation and to cast out devils. This is when I learned about spiritual warfare. God provided multiple opportunities to pray with and counsel others in the Word of God despite the state of my life.

In Louisiana, I learned who I was meant to be. I never thought I would be strong enough to endure what I was going through, but, through Christ, I was. One late, late night, one of Ben's "others" called my phone looking for him. He wasn't with me. He wasn't with her. I guess she was trying to upset me so I would leave him. I was not angry. I did not curse her out. I told her that she was better than that, and she was living beneath her privilege. I told her God had better for her, but she was being led of the devil. I also told her that what she was doing would never prosper, and she was bringing a curse on her head. She apologized and never called again.

All I wanted was peace. I was having dream after dream of Ben dying, and I was scared for him. I had been telling him the brutal truth for weeks, that if he continued to walk after the flesh he would die — whether that was spiritual or natural I didn't know. I pleaded with him to stop with the affairs and drugs and hanging around where he should not, but he thought I was mad at him and trying to speak death over him. Eventually, God said I could go back home to Illinois. I was so excited. And God provided! A family member sent me money, and my husband actually gave me the majority of his paycheck. I packed up everything I could fit in my Corolla with my two babies (Ben helped me pack the car too…won't God do it?) I tossed my wedding dress in the dumpster without a backward glance, and I hit the highway.

I arrived back in Illinois on December 31st. I would have found a lawyer the next day, but it was New Year's Day. By January 2nd, God had already told me not to take my ring off. I was not happy about that at all. Here it was, I'm back in Illinois, ready to start my life as a single mom and put my stupid mistakes behind me, and God says "No!" I was so angry! I was mad at my husband…AND God!! I just wanted to be free to start over and live a life of peace! I knew that if I couldn't take my ring off, I couldn't divorce my husband. God had something up his sleeve! Then God said, "Pray for your husband." I politely told God I didn't want to, but he quickly reminded me of the grace and mercy I had received and how my husband needed prayer. Who was I to withhold it? Looking back now as I write this, I realize that my husband would have received God's grace, because God is grace, and He loves His children enough to chase them. He told me to pray for Ben for my sake, so that the poison of bitterness would not kill me. It is impossible to pray for someone sincerely and have no compassion in your heart for them. I prayed out of obedience, and God helped me understand that there are souls that are going to go to hell if they don't turn from their wicked ways. Some people need help, prayer help, to get to a place of repentance. This is called intercession. We should not want even our worst human enemy to go to hell. Despite what the world may think, the literal place of hell is very real.

As I prayed for my husband, God was healing my heart. He helped me see my flaws (so I would learn from them) as well as my positives (so I might grow in them). He renewed my strength and delivered me from the generational curse of divorce. He took my brokenness and restored my faith, hope, joy and love. As God worked on me, he was also working on my husband. Ben rededicated his life to God, moved to Illinois, and established himself as a keyboardist in our home church. During our healing period, he lived in a motel, got a job in construction, spent time with the kids on weekends and respected my boundaries. I say that because he initially determined that I had to forgive him because the bible says so. He felt I needed to trust that he was okay because he said he was okay. He wanted to just move on like he did not put a dagger through my heart! My determination was to never again go through what we had gone through. I told him that when God cleared him and told me to go back to him, I would. Other than that, I was not entertaining any ideas of getting back together. The phrase I often used and still use is that "You found me in God, you'll keep me in God." This again, is a testimony of God having built up my faith. I'd love to tell you that I was good and was not concerned about what the future held for us, but that would be an outright lie. I was straight up trusting God. As I said before, when God told me not to take my wedding ring off, I knew he wanted us back together. God had a plan in mind for US; I just didn't know what it was. And he never said serving Him wouldn't be a sacrifice; in fact, He said it would be (Romans 12:1). But He promised that all things would work out for my good (Romans 8:28). I loved God and chose to do his divine will. I loved Ben and chose to honor my wedding vows to him.

My husband and I reconciled after six months of separation. We courted all over again and worked on rebuilding our friendship. We talked a lot (he made himself accountable to me by calling whenever he was away). And we both decided that divorce would not be an option for us. We bought a home, welcomed more children and often strategized how we might move our family forward spiritually, financially and emotionally. We also set ground rules for discussions which is very important for any successful marriage. The rules were set to help us talk about things that were difficult to talk about. It was meant to give each person a safe space to reveal their heart. The rules we set were as follows:

Rule #1- Listen while the other person is talking. Do not interrupt them. Don't make assumptions or accusations but ask for clarity with items that are not understood. Don't mentally rehearse your rebuttal while they are talking, because that means you are not listing. Give them your undivided attention.

Rule #2- Keep your tone calm during discussions even if something is said that you don't like. Anger does not resolve issues but adds fuel to an already kindled fire.

Rule #3- Don't hit below the belt by saying words with the intent to cut or damage the other person. You can't un-ring a bell. What you say should edify or correct, but not kill. Speak the truth in love, but don't hurt others because you are hurting.

Rule #4- Believe in the good (and the God) in your spouse. Right or wrong, they are not your enemy. Don't condemn them. God will judge the right and wrong if both of you cannot agree on an issue.

Rule #5- Table the discussion if things get too heated or get out of hand. Know when to shut up! Pray for peace and wisdom. Don't let pride cause a rift where there does not need to be one.

As a kindergarten teacher, it is so very necessary to have a few simple rules for the classroom. The rules can't be too complicated or too numerous…not if you want Kinders to know and follow them. They can't be responsible for doing what they can't retain. Same in a marriage. Have a few simple rules of engagement that are impactful if followed as directed! Post them as reminders if necessary. That way, you and your spouse can consciously keep that flesh in control, and you won't clown when you should be communicating. My hubby and I diligently adhered to these rules for a while and did well, but like seasons, things changed. Ben backslid again. He couldn't escape the darkness. And this time, it consumed him!

9 | GET THE HELL OUT OF YOUR MARRIAGE

You ever had one of those plants that though you cut it down, it grows right back? That's how sin is! If you don't uproot it, it will keep coming back to wreak havoc in your life. It can lie dormant for a while to give you a false sense of security, then at the most inconvenient of times (anytime is an inconvenient time), it springs up to choke you out! Therefore, we should never hide our sins from God, ourselves or the ones we love. There may be times where you are not sure of what exactly is hidden in the recesses of your heart. Thankfully, Jesus is the Light of the World and is more than gracious to reveal the darkness within us so that we can get rid of it. Uproot that mess and be fully and totally free!

After our reconciliation, Ben and I talked about some of our prior issues but did not delve into deep things not wanting to sabotage our newfound peace.

In time, when we finally discussed some touchy issues, we broke the ground rules we had established for discussions. Old hurts resurfaced and fresh wounds cut deep. We learned to function in disfunction (that's another bible class). We allowed hell to remain, because it seemed easier than fighting for our liberty. I didn't have the fears that I had before we separated, but I was tired of the roller coaster of emotions and the mental anguish that characterized our marriage. I was tired of fighting and feeling like the end was nowhere in sight. But God strengthened me for THIS journey. He created me to be strong and courageous. He gave me THIS husband, and so He was responsible for helping me love the hell out of him. God encouraged me with scriptures like "delight thyself also in the Lord: and he shall give thee the desires of thine heart" (Psalm 37:4). And "ye have need of patience, that, after ye have done the will of God, ye might receive the promise" (Hebrews 10:36).

When I say God was talking to me and gave me an understanding of how all things are connected. My God! When God makes "love connections", they are according to his heart because God knows what we have need of before we can ask or think. God chose me for Ben because I am strong. I could endure what was going on with him because of my love for God. I surrendered to God, and he strengthened me for Ben. I didn't understand initially what God was doing, but I trusted God not to let me die in the fire. I needed Ben for patience, boldness and compassion. Ben needed me for unconditional love, acceptance and faith. I had to fight for my husband, because he needed me to stand in the gap for him. He told me later that many would have walked away long ago, but I stayed. God ordained me to stay. The enemy fought hard for me to walk away from Ben, our marriage, and the destiny that I did not foresee, but God was for US!

The bible says in Ephesians 2:4-5, "But God, who is rich is mercy, for his great love wherewith he loved us, even when we were dead in sins, hath quickened us together with Christ, (by grace ye are saved) and hath raised us up together and made us sit together in heavenly places in Christ Jesus". Notice how many times "together" is mentioned. We must be in this thing together. No man is an island to himself. The bible also says, "two is better than one… and a threefold cord is not quickly broken" (Ecclesiastes 4:9,12). My husband needed a strong woman to endure hardness with him…to pray him through to his purpose, to our purpose. Now let me tell you this! You can only do this as directed by God! I am not talking about dealing with somebody's mess because you don't want to live without them. This is not being tolerant of someone's infidelities and foolishness because you have no value in yourself. This is not being used as a doormat because you don't want to be alone. No ma'am! No sir! I was on assignment!! God would not let me fail, because I said yes to the assignment, and I surrendered to Him in love. Am I saying that Ben could not be saved without me? Goodness no! But God sets all things up the way He does because He knows what and WHO we need. That's why it is so important to know you are with whom God has appointed for you. It's about so much more than just you. It's about your spouse, your children, your purpose and any to whom God sends you.

My husband's rebellion led him to consume alcohol and pills and to flatline on an emergency room table. Despite warnings from God, me and others, he would not believe God's truth for his life...that he was loved, that he was worth Christ's sacrifice, and that he was made for greatness. Whatever is not of faith is sin, and the wages of sin is death. But Glory be to God for His mercy that brought Ben back, and the prayers of the righteous that availed much!

There were many underlying factors that resulted in my husband's backsliding. I will not get into all of that for privacy reasons, but for the sake of this book, I will reveal three "roots" that overtook our marriage from the start:

Root #1- "The Other Guy". It was a bone of contention between us. Ben felt like sloppy seconds. He thought I wished I was with the other guy. I married Ben, but it's like he couldn't receive that I was with him by choice. He said and did things, in my opinion, to push me away. When I pulled away from him emotionally and physically, that just gave credence to his thought that I didn't want to be with him. No matter what I said to him or what I did for him, he just could not fathom that I loved and wanted him. The spiritual root of his issue was rejection and low self-worth which was planted in him in his childhood.

Root #2- "The Sex Issue". He wanted it and I tolerated it. I had closed myself off from him. I felt so wounded by his words and actions that I allowed myself to become numb. In my mind, I couldn't trust him with my heart, so how could I give him my body? I am not excusing my actions, but simply declaring my mindset at the time. There was no intimacy outside of the bedroom (he was typically gone), but then he would criticize me or accuse me when I did have sex with him because I wasn't "into it". He didn't understand that I was trying, so I stopped. There were times when he tried to romance me, but I didn't trust it to be genuine. I thought it a means to get me to drop my guard. The infidelities were hurtful, but, to me, the whole process of trying to love Ben had become torture. He was deceived and tormented. He thought God wanted to kill him and that I hoped he would die. He thought he was a screw up and had been cursed by God. He thought nobody loved him, including his wife and his five children. The spiritual roots of this stem from a spirit of rejection and a spirit of despair.

Root #3- "Religion, not Relationship". When Ben and I married, we both had a surface understanding of God. We went to church, paid our tithes and offerings and worked in whatever capacity we were asked or desired to. But our understanding was not sufficient for where God was taking us. We had to know that He was the Lily of the valley. We had to know that the name of the Lord is a strong tower and the righteous run into it and are safe. We had to know that we could take a few knocks and not weaken in our love for God or each other. We were tried immediately after our wedding, and, per worldly standards, should have called it quits not long after that. But God was going to be glorified! He wanted us to know Him, that He is sovereign in our life, that what He has planned, He will perform. The bible says that we learn obedience by the things that we suffer. God was looking for us to defy the odds and obey his will. Religion allows you to sin and justify yourself. Religion consents to you doing your own will and then tell you God understands. Religion accepts God's Word but does not necessarily follow it. But God tells us that obedience is greater than sacrifice (1 Samuel 15:22). "What doth the Lord require of thee, but to do justly, and to love mercy, and to walk humbly with thy God" (Micah 6:8). Do what's right and LOVE MERCY!! When is mercy necessary but when someone wrongs you? Also think of that scripture where Jesus told the disciples to forgive seventy times seven...why would he say that but that He knows folks are going to do you wrong? He has given you of his forgiveness (and strength) to forgive others no matter what. Jesus was the role model for forgiving heinous crimes and offences against our person. This is no less valid in a marriage with the wife or husband that is the closest thing to you but acting as your enemy. FORGIVE and give God glory!

So here are some concise steps that you can take to get the hell out of your marriage. It will take courage and honesty, but nothing is too hard for God or you!

1) ACKNOWLEDGE YOUR ROLE IN WELCOMING THE HELL.

Don't point fingers. Don't make a list of wrongs the other person did. Acknowledge YOUR part in any breakdowns in the marriage. I will be very candid here about ME. There were some things that I did that exacerbated the problems in our marriage. First off, I did not accept my husband as my head. He was younger in age, and I had been saved longer. When he moved in with me, I wanted things a certain way. When he got laid off, I had to be the bread winner. When I asked him how we were going to proceed from that point, he didn't seem to have a plan. I felt like I couldn't depend on him for much, and I lost respect for him.

Secondly, I was selfish. I felt like my husband was there to treat me like a princess (here goes that fairy tale stuff again). That's what happened in the movies (those movies are named after the female, are they not?), so I wanted my marriage to be all about me and my desires. I wanted to be happy. I wanted my husband to adore me and be totally devoted to me. I wanted him to do whatever he needed to do to assure that I was not stressed or worried about anything. Our sexual issues were a painful reminder that I can't control everything, and my body was not just my own. I needed to learn to share and play nice. The world didn't rotate around me! I am not taking blame for my husband's affairs (he made the choice to do what he did), nor minimizing the high sexual demand that was upon me in the beginning of my marriage (he was delivered from a lust spirit), but I am simply saying that the scene was set for sin. The devil played his part, and so did I. I helped let the hell in. I aided the enemy in the demise of my marriage. I had wanted to be perfect, but I was far from it. Before God's revelation, I was religious. I had seen my husband as a "situation" and not a soul. For years, I doubted God had a purpose for my pain.

2) <u>REPENT</u>.

In that first three months of our separating, I felt very justified in my anger and stance for wanting a divorce. I continually told God how hurt I was and how Ben had done me so wrong. I told God that if he loved me, he would allow me to be free of this man. I became as the Pharisee who was praying and said,

"God, I thank thee, that I am not as other men are, extortioners, unjust, adulterers, or even as this publican" (Luke 18:11). I was self-righteous. The bible says before you can remove a mote from your brother's eye, consider the beam that is in your own (Matthew 7:3-5). I became an offense to God with my selfishness and pride. When God brought this to my attention, it pricked my heart. I was so busy recounting my husband's errors that I was not aware of how I was condemning him, how I had become an accuser of the brethren, how I was hating someone that I can see, while saying I love God whom I could not see. I repented. I could have held on to all the hurt and anger and bitterness, but I let it go for Christ's sake and my sake. Jesus loved me; he bled and died not just for me but for all. How can I tell God that I was worth it, but make it seem like my husband was not? From the moment of my repentance, not only did I see myself through the eyes of grace, but I saw Ben in a different light. No matter his troubles, he was a child of God. I had no heaven or hell to put him in and by whatever measure I judged him (or anyone else), the same would be measured to me. Jesus was the ultimate example of forgiving those that despitefully used and abused him. So, I too had to get this lesson. For the servant is not greater than his master. This was a humbling lesson but also very liberating. I began to laugh again and know joy again and thank God again instead of always complaining. His love is unfailing.

That's what He wants us to exude…unfailing love!

3) <u>ALLOW GOD TO HEAL YOU</u>!

Oftentimes we are focused on the other person and what they are or are not doing or feeling. Loose it and let it go! Jesus asked Peter three times if he loved Him and then Jesus let Peter know what he would experience by following Him. Peter wanted to know what John was going to do. Jesus succinctly responded, "You follow me!" Yes, this is what we need to keep our focus on…following Jesus! It is none of our business what God is doing with someone else. Let Him handle that. It will be a distraction to you anyway. No! You focus on the Lord! Let him speak to you. Let him pour in the oil and the wine. Let him apply the healing salve that will mend your heart and soul. In this way, no matter what the other party chooses to do (again, they have a choice) you will be made whole. You will come out wiser and stronger than when you went in and when it is time to reconcile, you will be ready. If the other party chooses not to reconcile, the Bible says in 1 Corinthians 7:15, that "if the unbelieving depart, let them depart, for God has called you to peace".

We must remember that our purpose for being down here is not to be married, but to do a work for the Lord, to bring glory to His name! The enemy will use anything and anyone to hinder you from fulfilling the purpose of God, and your stance must be "as for me and my house we will serve the Lord" (Joshua 24:15). No matter the trials or troubles that come your way, stay with the Lord. There was a woman in the bible that had an issue of blood for twelve years, and she squandered all she had trying to be healed. It was not until she came to Jesus, crawling on the ground through a crowd of people, that she was made whole. Oh, how she wanted to be healed of her affliction! How badly do you want to be healed? Do you care more for appearances, or do you truly want an answer for your problem? The Bible states, "But seek ye first the kingdom of God, and his righteousness; and all these things shall be added unto you" (Matthew 6:33). That includes in marriage! Paul said the marriage is supposed to be a representation of Christ and the church (Ephesians 5:32), so how much the more would God be willing to fix you, your spouse and your marriage if you put him first.

4) DON'T ALLOW LIES TO TAINT THE TRUTH.

Many of us stood before a multitude of people and swore before God and everybody that this was our boo till death do us part. We swore to love, honor and cherish them and be true and faithful to them right in front of that mighty cloud of witnesses. Uh-huh, you didn't know the enemy was going to come after you to make you eat your words, did you? He wants to make a liar out of you and sadly it doesn't take much. The bible admonishes in Mark 10:9, "What therefore

God hath joined together, let not man put asunder."
Some like to think there is some hidden disclaimer
down the road when all hell is breaking loose, and
they say, "Well, God didn't tell me to marry
him/her." Well, then you're a liar! What about the
engagement process, the marriage license, the
wedding planning, the family celebrations, etc.? So,
all of that was on a whim? It meant nothing? You had
nothing better to do? No, you made a choice! You
made a commitment, but when the bottom falls out,
you want to blame the other person or irreconcilable
differences for why the marriage did not work. You
either did not seek God for clarity regarding your
spouse before you got married, or you did not care
what God had to say so you ignored any warning
signs, or you were in direct rebellion when you clearly
heard God say no, and you said yes anyway. You
don't get a pass! Don't blame it on ignorance. Take
responsibility for YOUR actions. Own up to your
error. If you don't learn from your mistakes, you're
bound to repeat them.

Also, don't run the other spouse down. That makes
you look foolish. Again, you stood before the masses
and said "I do" but then you want to tear them down
when you *don't* anymore. That is childish and
arrogant! They can still be a good person (maybe even
better) without you if you are not willing to change.
Have you ever wondered about people who have
been married multiple times who always have an evil

report about their former spouses? My question is, "Who is the common denominator?" All of them can't be wrong! And if the former spouses got together to discuss that person, what would they all say?

Friends, if a person is good enough for you to marry (yes, it is okay to be honest if they are lazy or trifling or mean-spirited or whatever), but don't condemn them to make yourself look or feel better. This is especially crucial if they are the father/mother of your children. That is bringing hell into your house and a curse on your head and creating generational curses for your own children. Remember that love covers all kinds of sins, so cover your spouse in prayer! And what happens if you run them down to everybody, then they get right and the two of you decide to reconcile? Now you and your spouse must wade through all the bad reports that you put out there. Again, YOU will look like a fool. If your spouse was so horrible, why were you with them? You leave no room for redemption when you talk down about your husband or wife. And you also begin to believe all the bad things that you are saying about them, magnifying the bad and nullifying the good that they may have done. You should say "The truth is the marriage fell apart because I ___" (you fill in the blank). Own your part. Bite your chunk even if it was the fact that you did nothing and watched it unravel to the end.

Are there instances where clearly wrong was done

to you? Sure! For instance, you may have experienced physical, mental, verbal abuse, etc.? Even then, ask yourself-- How did I get here? What drew me to this person and this person to me? Why did I ignore all the flags/warnings? Why did I not speak up sooner when I saw things that were off or not right? Did I want to be married so bad that I sacrificed myself and my peace of mind? How can I break this stronghold so that it never happens again? What is in me that is so broken that I attract people that want to hurt me? Why did I feel that I was not worth more? Such questions will lead to the soul searching necessary for healing and deliverance. Again, if you don't heal, you will go through these cycles again and again. Or sad still, you'll find a good person but will dog them out because you are the common denominator in dysfunctional relationships. This is the will of the devil, but certainly not the will of God.

5) RISE UP AND WALK.

Gone are the days of passivity and putting your Christian journey on cruise control. You have to take authority over your life and the things of your domain. We have power over all the enemy's power (Luke 10:19). We must hold fast to the word of God and the principles of God. There is no way to walk in healing if you don't get up and actively participate in your progress. This means you can't keep doing the same things you've always done and think you'll get different results. No more complaining and being negative about situations you don't like or don't want to do. Don't demean your spouse or allow doubts of failure to infiltrate your mind. The bible encourages us to hope in God (Psalm 42:11). Trust God to not only deliver you but to keep you delivered! God will keep your mind when your mind is stayed on Him. It can seem scary only because it requires you to be vulnerable (open) to God. Remember that fear is not from God. You must be willing to work for what you want, and you must do your part to see it happen. If you're not a communicator, learn to communicate. If you are always talking, learn how to be quiet and listen sometimes. Don't jump to conclusions. And do not allow the mess and muck of the past to creep back up and hinder your progress. The enemy constantly reminded me of my husband's infidelities when we first reunited, but I had to resist him. I chose to believe in God's love for me and my husband's renewed faithfulness to God and myself. It was difficult in the beginning, but Jesus healed my heart day by day and gave me this promise: "He is a rewarder of them that diligently seek him" (Hebrews 11:6). He is with me and thereby I am not alone. In this life (including in marriage) you shall have tribulation, but be of good cheer, Christ has already overcome the world and through him you and your spouse will too!

10 | GOD'S GRAND PLAN FOR US

Trouble don't last always! Thank God for that! There is a beginning and there is an end to situations in your life. If you go in, know that you will come out! When Jesus says, "Let us go to the other side" like he said to his disciples in Luke 8:22, you might face a storm or two, but you WILL get to the other side! The enemy wants to discourage us by making us feel hopeless and helpless, like we are at the mercy of the elements (circumstances) of life. But the devil is a big, fat, ugly LIAR!! God is the Author and Finisher of our faith. Only HE gets to dictate what shall or shall not be in our life!

When my husband died, God revived him. He also revived our marriage. Out of the many years my husband had been saved, he did not really understand God's love for him. He didn't believe God really could love him despite all he had done. But when God brought him back, he got the revelation. Instead of living a life of self-destruction, because he felt defeated by condemnation, he surrendered his life to God and followed him with all his heart. He became a prayer warrior and a devoted musician. Then God began to elevate him in the house of God and in our home.

God raised my husband up and set him in his rightful place as head of the family. I say "set" because some think it is an understood that this is what happens when a man gets married. However, like Adam, if he does not "take" dominion, another (the devil) will. How can he take dominion if he has no idea what that means? What does that entail and how does one do it? This is where counseling and male mentorship comes in. In addition, a man will abuse his power as head if he is not submitted to God. How can he lead his family in righteousness, if he is not following the Lord? Are there good men out there living by good moral standards? Many would say yes, but the steps of a good man are ordered by the Lord according to Psalm 27:33. So, by God's standards, a man that is obedient to his commands is a "good" man. This is another criterion to take into consideration when praying regarding your spouse. This, of course, is where prayer and study of the Word of God is invaluable. If a gentleman has a relationship with God before he meets his significant other, then a lot of shenanigans can be avoided because he will already know who he is and where he is going in God. When my husband became the head after God restored him, I submitted myself to him as his wife. It didn't happen overnight, but it did happen. I saw his walk with God. I witnessed his fruit of righteousness. He had been renewed in the spirit of his mind (Ephesians 4:23). He had power, praise and purpose! He was submitted and committed to God! He wasn't running from his calling anymore but running to it! And I was connected to the call! Submitting as a wife aided me in submitting myself to him as my pastor when we started the church years later (this step is vital in keeping hell out of the House of God).

As my husband loved on God, he learned to love me. He was attentive and present. He was compassionate and patient. He was driven and fun-loving again. I cherished this new husband. And you know God could not give me a new husband and not give him a new wife. When I say I was so ready to be new! Glory! My fears were replaced with faith! My sorrows were replaced with joy! My passivity was replaced with power! I absolutely loved God and my husband. I am in awe of what God did. I matured during my sojourn in the wilderness. I am stronger, wiser, bolder and braver! I don't have the fears I had before, because I know who I am, and I know my God! He is mighty! He never fails! He never forsakes!

There are going to be experiences that may be intimidating at first because it is unfamiliar, but God is with us through them all! In Him, we live and move and have our being (Acts 17:28)! God not only has a plan for us (think again on Jeremiah 29:11), but He has mapped it out and made provision for every circumstance. Out of all the souls on the planet, Noah and his family were the only ones saved from the flood. God had asked Noah to build an arc, despite the fact that it had never rained or that he may never have built a birdhouse let alone an arc. But God provided (he even sent the animals to Noah for preservation)! Noah could have thought it all foolishness, but he obeyed. Fighting for your marriage is like God asking you to build an arc (a fortified structure for your family that will withstand the elements from above and beneath). It's a large and laborious task that may make no sense to you. Everybody else is doing what they want to do; why do you have to do this? Because God wants to work a miracle in you and in your marriage! He wants to save others through the testimony of your lives! "For the eyes of the LORD run to and fro throughout the whole earth, to shew himself strong in the behalf of them whose heart is perfect toward him" (2 Chronicles 16:9).

My husband and I went through hell to do the work we are doing now for the Lord. In 2016, God called my husband and I to start a ministry in Belleville, IL. We are the Pastor and First Lady of Redeeming Love of Christ Church in Belleville, IL. The thing is…we are in this thing TOGETHER! That was God's plan—that we work together to disciple souls for Christ and encourage them to relationship, not religion! To teach them of God's redemption and love and that all things are possible with Him! To be living witnesses of God's grace and encourage the saints to walk fearlessly in the delivering power of God! This was God's plan for us all along, we just didn't know it. Why? Because we were so caught up in our dramas and desires and looked at marriage from a carnal point of view. This is a limited and base viewpoint that limits the faith of the people of God and aids in the derail of our divine destiny. God is very deliberate in his "couple" connections, because He knows which pairings will perpetuate the advancement of His kingdom and will adversely impact the enemy's kingdom. On the flip, the enemy promotes connections with decoys that block or abort your purpose. He wreaks havoc with divine connections to deviate them from God's plan. The latter is what the enemy tried with Ben and me, but he did not succeed! Ladies and Gentlemen, stay the course and keep the faith! God will uphold his Word. His word will not return to him void. Dig down deep and get some gumption in you! Don't lay down thinking it will all be over soon. That thief is trying to take what belongs to you! Put him out!

God has healed Ben and me. Our marriage is better than it ever was. We are on one accord as we should be in God. We love spending time together, in fact one of our things we do is drive around and talk or sit and talk in the car outside the house just to get some alone time (we have four boys at home ranging in ages, so we have to be creative). We are best friends and great supporters of one another. We seldom disagree, but should we come to a challenging discussion, we pray and trust our Father to give clarity. We are patient with each other and see the good in each other. And the sex! I'll put it this way: We are delightfully opportunistic with each occasion we are afforded to express our divine love connection. Come on, God!!

So, what is the conclusion of this whole matter? You and your spouse should be best friends. In fact, that's what most couples say they are before they get married. Then all of a sudden, the marriage and the friendship is null and void. But remember your vows. Remember the Lord that bought you. Remember your covenant with God, and he will help you keep the covenant you made with your spouse. Don't be selfish and self-serving. Don't throw one another under the bus because you are having a bad day. Pray for one another. Speak kindly to one another. Help one another be a better version of yourselves. There is so much more to life than fighting and being at odds with each other. The bible reminds us in 1 Peter 3:7 that we are "heirs together of the grace of life; that your prayers be not hindered." Seek to see the bigger picture (God's grand plan)!

If there is something that is not right or not working, work together to change it. Don't throw the baby out with the bath water. Don't trash your marriage and sabotage your spouse or yourself. Divorce should never be an easy option if you allow it to be an option at all. Jesus said that a decree of divorce was given because of the hardness of the people's hearts. As saints of God, our hearts should not be hard, but supple in the hands of the Master. We should be willing to do whatever it takes to please our God (notice I did not say our spouse; pleasing our spouse is a natural offshoot of pleasing the Lord). The main issue you will have to deal with is the hurt that comes along with a tumultuous marriage. You may wonder--How do I stop hurting? When will I stop hurting? How can I love over or through the hurt? The answer-- Jesus! Trust Jesus with every aspect of your marriage. "For it is God which worketh in you both to will and to do of his good pleasure" (Philippians 2:13). You and your spouse are a part of God's master plan. When you say yes to His will, He will provide the means and motivation to assist in your success. He will heal your wounds and remove any residue of pain and sorrow. Then, when you are whole, He will use YOU AND YOUR SPOUSE to build His glorious kingdom. So don't be afraid to get the hell out of your marriage!

REFERENCES

1. Cinderella and Snow White are stories in public domain.
2. Barbie, Ken, Barbie's Dream House and Barbie's Corvette are all products and exclusive trademarks of Mattel.
3. Easy Bake Oven is a registered trademark of Hasbro.
4. Rob Reiner, et al. A FEW GOOD MEN. USA, 1992.
5. The Temptations. "My Girl." The Temptations Sing Smokey, Robinson and White, 1964.
6. Oxford Languages online. Language data is provided by Oxford Press, part of Oxford University Press.
7. Kirk Franklin. "My Life is in Your Hands." God's Property from Kirk Franklin's Nu Nation, Franklin, 1997.
8. Merriam-Webster Online. Merriam-Webster, 2011.
9. LaShun Pace. "I Know I Been Changed". He Lives, Pace, 1991.

ABOUT THE AUTHOR

 Yvette Pete is the wife of Pastor Benjamin Pete and First Lady of Redeeming Love of Christ Church in Belleville, IL. She and Pastor Pete have been married for close to 24 years. They have been the leaders of RLCC for almost 6 years but have been ministering in various facets of kingdom work, including music ministry, youth ministry, evangelism, deliverance and couples counseling for over 20 years. They have five children and one grandchild.

LOOK FOR THESE UPCOMING INSPIRATIONAL TITLES BY YVETTE A. PETE

Good, Clean Sex
A Believer's Guide to True Intimacy
(September 2022)

The Call
A Believer's Guide to Embracing God's Purpose
(February 2023)

Made in the USA
Monee, IL
24 March 2022